MY MOST POWERFUL WEAPON

Dr. Florence Lightbourne Parra

 www.trafford.com

North America & international
toll-free: 1 888 232 4444 (USA & Canada)
phone: 250 383 6864 ♦ fax: 812 355 4082

Dedication

This book is dedicated to the men in my life:

My husband, Joseph Parra, whose patience and encouragement helped to bring it to completion. My love and gratitude to you for your understanding and for the design of the book cover.

My sons, Joel Howell and Jamel Howell who have been my inspiration and reason for continual growth and development.

My grandsons, Judah and Josiah Howell whom I pray will let prayer be the tool for navigating through this life.

My brother, David Lightbourne who has been the initial financial resource for my academics.

A Poem by a Granddad to His Unborn Grandchild.

I am sorry I cannot attend today,
But I have no time for play.
My work is to complete my worldly form,
Before I enter Life's perilous storm.

It is nice to know that someone is near,
Mom says everyone here is very dear.
Without your help she would be lost,
She could not have carried the emotional cost.
I thank you for providing Mom support,
What she owes to you she cannot report.

Dad thinks I'll come at the right time,
I will be able to hear the Christmas chime.
The beautiful tales of Christ's Birth,
And all the love upon this earth.
Thanks again for all this care,
Look forward to seeing you, soon as I dare

Much love, Baby Sanchez

Written by Joseph Arnold Parra (12/1990)

Contents

Acknowledgement

I give thanks and praise to God for my sisters who labor with me in the Gospel. They have been most diligent in critiquing my work and holding me accountable to the Gospel task of the message.

Grace and peace be unto you Bardine Hicks and Francis Hickman Jones, my faithful armor bearers and reviewers.

Grace and peace to my dearly beloved husband and prayer partner whose patience and understanding was vital to the review and completion of this book.

Blessing to all my prayer partners; you know who you are. I rely heavily on the prayers of my sisters and brothers in Christ.

Preface

Emmanuel

This book is written through the power of the Holy Spirit. It is my second inspiration from God to write a message to all who read. Those with ears let them hear. The book is written to let the world know that we wrestle not against flesh and blood but against principalities, against wickedness in high places. (Ephesians 6:12).

Christians are fighting a spiritual battle. Spiritual battles are not fought with knives and guns. It is impossible to cut out hate with human instruments. There is no scientific medicine that cures immorality and maliciousness. There is no surgical operation that can transform an evil heart to a heart of love. Spiritual weapons are the essential tools for spiritual battles.

Prayer is the weapon that moves the hands of God. The effectual fervent prayer of a righteous man availeth much. (James 5: 16). Prayer does what nothing else can do and what no one else can. Prayer is the tool of the saints. Prayer is the incense that goes up before God letting Him know that we recognize His sovereign power. It is our way of letting God know that we are dependent on Him and that we recognize His power and His Lordship. Prayer speaks to our humbleness and reminds us of our finiteness and God's infiniteness.

Prayer does the impossible, when we have exhausted all that is within our natural ability we will find that prayer opens the gate of human impossibility. God may work through natural means but He specializes in things that we think are impossible. God is a supernatural power that goes beyond what we can ever ask or phantom. God will do abundantly above that which we could ever ask or think. "Now unto Him that is able to do exceeding abundantly above all that we ask or think, according to the power that worketh in us." (Ephesians 3:20).

Therefore as you read this book I pray that you will make God your first response to life situations, whether they are good or bad. I pray that Jesus Christ will be your first response in every situation, not your last resort. That in emergencies before dialing 911 you will dial 111, one for the Father, one for the Son, and one for the Holy Spirit. Jesus wants to be our first choice in everything.

Remember when all else fails, God is there.
...and, lo, I am with you always, even unto the
end of the world. Amen. (Matthew 28:20)

MY
MOST
POWERFUL
WEAPON

"My Thoughts are not your Thoughts and
My Ways are not your Ways".

(Isaiah 55:8)

Chapter 1

God's mysterious ways

"And why can't I be a priest?" "Because only men are priests," replied my Anglican priest. "It's just not fair," I complained. "Well, you could join the convent that is designed for women," he said. "Well I guess so if that is my only choice," I replied. So I went in pursuit of what I felt was a "call" on my life. At 17 years old, I was excited that God would allow me to dedicate my life to Him by becoming a nun. This was short lived as my parents refused to sign the necessary papers that allowed a minor admittance to the convent. They told me I was too young to go into such a life and I needed more "discernment." Perhaps my parents had a vision that I could not see, surely they had good reasons.

I trusted my mom. She was my guiding light. In those days (the sixties) and in my country parents did not have to explain to their children the reasons for their decisions. Children respected their parents. We were taught to live by the instructions in Ephesians 6:1. "Children, obey your parents in the Lord: for this is right. Honor thy father and mother; which is the first commandment with promise; that it may be well with thee and thou mayest live long on the earth". Today this still remains God's pattern for my life.

I simply honored my parents and pursued another profession. I became a nurse. Everyone was happy and I guess, like Saint Paul, I learned to be content in whatever situation I found myself. Nursing became not just a profession, but a vocation. I found joy in ministering to people I came in contact with at work, the patients, and their families. In this profession I was able to minister to the physical body as well as to the spiritual being.

God does work in mysterious ways, His wonders to perform (See 1 Corinthians 1:25-31). In my final year of nursing school I met an ordained minister of the Gospel. After dating for a short while, he asked me to marry him. I accepted his marriage proposal. To me this was a sign from God that I was to be in what we call, "ordained" ministry. Why else would God send an ordained minister to ask for my hand in marriage?

We love to try and control things in our lives, which often cause us to forget who is in control. "For my thoughts are not your thoughts. . ." (Isaiah 55:8). The fact that I had not given any thought to marriage made this a praying time indeed. I loved my ministry and loved my professional work. I simply wanted to serve and dedicate my life to God. I needed no interruption, or so I thought. On this decision my parents allowed me to make my own choice.

Needless to say, this was not at all what I had envisioned for my life. Being denied the desire to enter the convent, finding joy in the profession of being a nurse, and now a marriage proposal was a bit much to digest. I had feelings of uncertainty regarding the proposal I prayed and fasted, but it seemed as if God was not listening, because I still had no answer. Using all the tools of my intellect, my reasoning skills, knowledge and emotions I consented to marriage. After all God sent me a preacher, this had to be His will. My answer was not necessarily God's answer.

As a result of petitioning God through prayer, He placed various persons before me. One such person was the leader of our Young Willing Workers Club; a woman who feared and dedicated her life to God, and her family. She was an inspiration. Her prayers and counsel gave me a new insight. Perhaps God was showing me, the ministry of wife and the role of mother was a greater work.

...Lean not to your own understanding...(Proverbs 3:5)

God supplies our needs according to His riches in Glory

(Philippians 4:19)

Chapter 2

The Struggle

A s intelligent human beings we have a tendency to think we know everything. Thus, we struggle with the mysteries of the kingdom. Why then do we struggle with the ways of Almighty God when He has made it plain? He clearly explains it for us in Isaiah 55:8-9. He did this to help us eliminate the anxiety of trying to figure out His ways. We, however, continue to struggle because we do not accept His words as written in Isaiah 55: 8-9. Let's take a look at what can cause us to struggle:

Lack of trust – We fear and are skeptical of the

unknown. Yet we claim to know Jesus, and the power of His love. If we look at our past, we will see that He has been faithful and should be reassured that we can lean and depend on Him. God always came through just when I needed Him most.

Lack of patience – We want God to act in a hurry on our time and to act in our way. He is a God you cannot hurry. There are some things, people, and situations we cannot change. We need wisdom to wait on God. *"Call unto me, and I will answer thee, and show thee great and mighty things, which thou knowest not."* (Jeremiah 33:3).

Self Control - As control freaks we want to manage and be in control of every situation. There are some situations that are beyond our control. So, get out of God's way and allow Him to do what no other power on earth can do. God specializes in things that humans think are impossible. We are to let go and let God have complete control.

Anxiety – We are anxious about everything, fear of the known and the unknown. Fear and anxiety hinder us and make us look to humans when we should look to God who works through human beings. Anxiety hinders our prayer and faith life. *"Be anxious for nothing, but in everything by prayer and supplication, with thanksgiving, let your requests be made known to God;*

and the peace of God, which surpasses all understanding, will guard your hearts and minds through Christ Jesus." (Philippians 4:6,7).

Ability – Education, reasoning skills and intellectual ability often interferes with divine intervention. Our analysis of the "facts" leaves little or no room for the working mysterious power of God. Problems are solved based on our ability, our reasoning skills or our academic opinion. "Trust in the Lord with all your heart, and lean not on your own understanding; in all your ways acknowledge Him, and He shall direct your paths." (Proverbs 3:5-6).

God will direct your path

Be anxious for nothing but all things by prayer and
supplication let your request be made known unto God.

(Philippians 4:6)

Chapter 3

My Struggle

"Oh, God where is he? He is never this late. It is 2:00 a.m. in the morning. My husband is not home. I am afraid. I am in a strange land. I am in the United States of America. My family is back in a small town on a small island, a place where everyone knows everyone. I don't know who to call. I have just moved here six months ago. I was all alone in a foreign land. I had no choice but to call on Jesus. Lord, help me. Give me peace; let me know if he is alright. Please bring him home safely. At 3:30 a.m. I hear the car roll into the driveway. I began to praise and thank the Lord that my husband had arrived home safely. My prayer was, "Thank you Lord for bringing peace to my spirit and for answering my prayers."

My husband and I both were professors of the Christian faith. I thought we were able to be honest with each other as we live out our faith. He apologized for not coming home at a decent hour and for not phoning to let me know he would be home late. He promised to call if he would be late or unable to make it home from what was called a "business encounter".

How ironic, within the same month I was standing at the same window, wondering the same thing and saying the same prayers. Where is he? Please Lord, bring Him home safely. This time he did not come home for three days. I began to pray more fervently. I was extremely worried because of the reported crime rates in America. I began to imagine all sorts of things that could have happened.

My fears led me to call the police and the neighboring hospitals. Neither the police nor the hospitals had reports of unidentified accident victims. I didn't know any of his friends. The members of the church had not heard from him. All I could do was call on Jesus. I prayed fervently and I prayed incessantly. I prayed like I had never prayed before. I was praying for one I dearly loved.

My husband returned home on the evening of the third day with no explanation. He did however apologize and promised not to repeat the behavior again. I accepted the apology and forgave. I must confess, forgetting was a bit more difficult. I began to pray for strength to forgive and forget. I prayed for wisdom to be true to my marriage vows and for patience as I learned what it meant, "until death do you part". I had to ask God to help me with my pride since I had only been married a short time and did not want the disgrace of a divorce. After all, we were Christians and great leaders in the community.

To my dismay, my husband's behavior did not change. There were more late nights, absent days and nights. It seemed as though God wasn't hearing my cries. Why God? Why did you bring me here, in a strange land to have me suffer like this? Why God are you not changing him? God help me. I cried and I prayed. I prostrated myself before God day and night. Lord please, don't let him go out tonight. Let him stay at home. Let him not be cheating on the marriage. Help Lord Jesus. Show me your way oh God. Lead me in the path of righteousness.

Satan will play havoc with your mind and soul if you let him. In the Book of John 10:10 it reads: "The thief comes only to steal and kill and destroy; I came that they may have life, and have it abundantly."

How does he attack? Through the mind. Satan will tell you, "What is good for the goose is good for the gander." It is a lie from hell. Satan will tempt you with discouragement and will try to attack your self-esteem. You begin to doubt yourself and think little of who you are. Am I not good enough? What is out there that is not at home. Am I ugly? Am I too skinny? I was very skinny; I weighed 105 pounds at that time. Do I need to be more sophisticated; after all I was the "First Lady".

If you let Satan, he will cause chaos with every inch of your being. If he could he would try to take your soul. Cause depression that can lead to suicide. But thanks be to God I did not allow Satan to dampen my spirit. I sought refuge in the Lord. I prayed the Word daily, three and four times a day. I relied on the scriptures for my strength. "I praise you because I am fearfully and wonderfully made . . . " Psalm 139:14.

I relied heavily on God's word of reassurance. Jeremiah 1:5 says: "Before I formed thee in the belly I knew thee; and before thou camest forth out of the womb I sanctified thee, [and] I ordained thee a prophet unto the nations." This scripture became a part of my everyday life for I needed affirmation that I was of value and my life was ordained for a divine purpose.

The word of God was my stabilizing fort. I needed self-esteem and affirmation of who I was in Jesus Christ. I had nowhere else to turn, nor anyone in whom I could confide. After all, my husband was the pastor of a very prominent church in the city and I would not defame his character. (Read Psalm 46:2)

Satan will not only play havoc with your mind, but also with your emotions. You begin to wonder

'What will people think?' I am too ashamed to go back home. I cannot handle the shame.

A great part of our defense is to know the various forms in which he may appear:

- Satan is An Adversary (1 Peter 5:8)
- A Tempter (1 Thessalonians 3:5)
- A Deceiver (2 Corinthian 11:3)
- A Hinderer (1 Thessalonians 2:18)
- A Beast (Revelation 19:19)
- A Restless Lion (1 Peter 5:8)
- The god of this world (2 Corinthians 4:4)
- Prince of the power of the air (Ephesians 2:2)

Prayer is the only weapon that is effective against our adversary the devil. Use it. It brings down strongholds. Read 2 Corinthians 10:4.

I can truly say, the struggles in my life taught me how to pray without ceasing. My life became a life of prayer. The prayer "God is our refuge and strength, an ever present help in trouble. (Psalms 46:1), was always on my lips. I prayed continuously.

In an attempt to change my husband and the situation, I begged and I threatened him to be true to our vows. I left a few times thinking that separation would help our marriage. I tried with everything within my power to control a humanly uncontrollable situation. When I began to realize that I could not change his behavior I began to let go and allow God to take charge. I no longer begged or pleaded with him.

I simply began to accept the things I could not change and allowed God to work in me.

After releasing the situation completely over to God I was able to sleep at night and not be bothered by my husband's absence. His behavior became his lifestyle and prayer became mine. I began to find courage and fortitude as God continued to work in me. God is so loving and so caring He simply waits for us to relinquish our struggles into His hands.

If you are going to worry don't pray. But if you are going to use your greatest weapon against worry pray. Turn your struggles over to the Lord He will take care of you.

It is better to trust in the Lord than
to put confidence in man

(Psalms 118:8)

God's power is made perfect in weakness:

(2 Corinthians 12:9)

Chapter 4

God's grace is sufficient.

God did a new thing in me. He brought to my attention that in every situation I was to trust Him. I did not attend any stress relief classes, nor did I engage in any 12-Step Programs, but I did engage in prayer warfare and I found that God's grace was sufficient.

God is gracious; He sent His angel to minister to me. He sent a 90 year old angel with wisdom and experience. She was known in the neighborhood as "Mama Jones." Mama Jones lived across the street from the church parsonage where we lived. She had the gift of discernment and the gift of wisdom.

She became a dear friend who sat with me through times of great distress. She always had a word of encouragement. She reminded me constantly that her age had afforded her much experience and her salvation much grace. Her advice to me was biblically sound. She said, "Be still and let God work in you." She was a welcomed presence during this troubled time in my life. She would quietly sit with me focusing not on my issues, but on the goodness of God. I praised God for allowing our paths to cross and for the companionship she provided to a foreigner who was in a strange land.

She became my Naomi. She encouraged me and gave me sound advice on using my time wisely. I was not eligible for employment in America at that time and she admonished me not to focus on myself, stay prayerful, and to think about what I could do for the Kingdom through the grace of God. Naomi was Ruth's mother-in-law. She encouraged Ruth to go to the fields and to glean. She also encouraged her to go into Boaz, her redeemer kinsman. She advised Ruth to do the right thing for the right reason so that she could be redeemed. Mama Jones kept me praying and kneeling at the feet of Jesus. She wanted me to do the right thing for the right reason. My faith was on trial. How could God bring me to a strange place and leave me alone? Where was God when I needed Him most?

I was reassured through my 90 year old angel that God's grace was with me and He had not forsaken me.

God's amazing grace truly kept me and showered me as I faced the struggles in my life. Through our prayer time together I began to feel the reassuring grace of God's presence which was strengthening me.

My husband and I moved to a large city where the bright lights and the big city went to my "baby's" head. Instead of the situation becoming better, things went from bad to worse. There was no commitment at home. The length of time my husband stayed away from home increased. The anonymous phone calls and the lies profoundly increased.

God was gracious unto me. I cannot stress enough to you, dear reader, that prayer became my last name. I needed a friend. God's grace kept me in Palmetto. God's grace kept me in Ohio. It is great to talk to God, but somehow I needed an earthly being (an angel) with flesh and blood. I needed encouragement from heaven. One who would not judge or criticize, but keep me focus on kingdom work and kingdom principles.

Ask and it shall be given. Seek and ye shall find. We need the prayers and strength of our sisters and brothers. God sent me wonderful friends who walked with me along the way in this struggle. There was Curlie, a God-fearing, Spirit-filled woman who encouraged me and always reminded me that God will take care of me. She was my "angel" in Ohio.

Over the years I have heard the saying, "A two-fold cord is not easily broken." Jesus sent His disciples out two by two and I often wondered why. I believe God wants us to work in teams. We are not in our battles alone. We are not the only one with issues or problems. Satan will easily deceive us into thinking so and that we are alone. But what a friend we have in Jesus. Ask Him for what you want, for what you need. He said, "If you call me I will answer. Call unto me, and I will answer thee, and shew thee great and mighty things, which thou knowest not." Jeremiah 33:3

God knows what you need, when you need it and how much you need. He is such a good and gracious Father. Unbeknownst to me He was preparing me for unseen situations further down the road. Don't ask me why. Just don't underestimate the power of almighty God. Nor scorn His handiworks. I don't know why Ruben and the other brothers sold Joseph. It certainly seemed like a bad day for Joseph, but God worked for their good and His glory. He will use situations for the edification of His kingdom. I know I am a witness of His goodness.

It may appear as if prayer will not change your situation, but it does. It will change how we react to situations; and it will change us into people who are dependent on God. Prayer changed my attitude. I was better able to cope with the behavior of my spouse as my inner man was strengthened. I began to grow in grace. I began to experience God in a new way. His grace sustained me. His response to my prayers was to increase my faith and to empower me in my prayer life. I can truly say God's grace is sufficient.

Paul prayed three times for God to remove the thorn from his flesh. God said, "My grace is sufficient." In the midst of struggles always remember to pray, it communicates our needs to God. Prayer is a means of grace.

Be careful for nothing; but in everything by prayer and supplication with thanksgiving let your requests be made known unto God.

(Philippians 4:6).

Yield yourself completely to Him,
Fully committed to His will and way.

(Psalms 37:5)

Chapter 5

My Desire

I worked as a registered nurse for 35 years and was employed by the State for over 19 years. My plans were to continue in my management position for a few more years and then retire with the great benefits that come from being a state employee. Note that I stated, "My plans."

God continued to speak to me regarding His plans for my life. For over five years God was giving me specific directions about His call on my life. I followed some, others I ignored. For example, I took the Clinical Pastoral Education (CPE) Program believing He was directing me to use my licensing and ordination (call to ministry) in the healthcare setting.

However, God's plan for my life was superseding my plans. He wanted me now! Nevertheless, I continued to ask God to let me keep my job as a nurse manager just a little while longer. Believe me, God's will, will be done. My job became uncomfortable. The cohesive work environment on the job seemed to break down. Betrayal by subordinates occurred. Physicians became disgruntled.

Regardless of what God was speaking to my heart, my plans were final. I knew what I wanted and nothing was going to stop me. I was going to do it my way. I tried with all in my power to do it my way. God will allow what ever is necessary to accomplish His will.

Here is a teaching moment for you dear reader. If or when you continue to turn a deaf ear on God's call for your life, He will take measures and move you forward to His will. One day I was given options--resign or be terminated. I had done nothing wrong. Nothing negative could be documented or substantiated about my work, but the handwriting was on the wall. My days were numbered. Had I simply listened to the voice of God and allowed myself to do his will, much pain and embarrassment would have been avoided.

But I was not quite willing to say, "Thy will be done" and truly mean it.

> *Therefore, whatever you want men to*
> *do to you, do also to them, ...*
>
> *(Matthew 7:12)*

Chapter 6

When the Die is cast

There is nothing you can do when the die is cast you cannot fight it. There is absolutely nothing you can do when God is in the plan. God works in mysterious ways His wonders to perform.

As I said earlier my plans were to work a few more years as a nurse and then retire and do mission work. God's will is above and beyond our will. God knew the plans He had for my life. *"...For I know the plans I have for you," declares the Lord, "Plans to prosper you and not to harm you, plans to give you hope and a future..." (Jeremiah 29:11)*. But how can this be I have my plans. I have a future in the Florida State Retirement system. What better system could one ask for? The heavenly system is far superior to the state system or any government system. I had to learn this the hard way.

The hospital was downsizing and requests for voluntary retirement, packages were offered. I took neither.

The die was cast. The political game was at work. I could see the injustices of the institutions. One physician who held great clout was not comfortable with the "nigger" unit, commonly referred to as the "N" unit or the "nigger" Nurse Manager and continued to talk to administration about my removal as Nurse Manager/Supervisor.

In the political arena the doctor has the greater stance whether working within the scope of practice or not. Administration, in my opinion did not want to make this doctor upset so naturally the person of lower status would not be catered to or protected. I was given the option of resignation or be placed on a work contract. Needless, to say a contract that even Superwoman would not be able to fulfill. Knowing all this, I still did not resign. Somehow I did not trust God. He just wasn't making sense to me. I only needed two years.

I would go to the hospital chapel and pray every chance I got. I would lay my request before God. I would say "God all I need is two more years". "God why aren't you listening to me" I did not want to have to find another State job. I just wanted to complete my service at the highest salary possible.

When God speaks, listen. He spoke most clearly. One morning as I entered my office, I was greeted by human resource and my superior who informed me that I was being let go. I wasn't mad at God after all He had been speaking to me telling me to resign. I failed to heed His voice. I was angry at the institution and the doctor. I had to reconcile myself with God and ask for his mercy in not listening and following His directions.

I was not worried about a job because RNs were needed everywhere – once again my own plans. I had to stop and seek direction. I said, "Lord. I know you asked me to resign, but I failed to do so. And now I am getting ready to go and apply for yet another job. Go with me and pave the way for me."

God did me one better. As I lay on my bed the phone rang. It was a job offer to be Director of Nurses for a conglomerate group of home healthcare agencies in the Tampa and St. Petersburg area. I was able to negotiate my salary. The job had excellent benefits that surpassed the benefits of the state job.

God has a sense of humor. Within one week on the job, the State Department showed up unannounced for state certification. I asked my assistant to take them into the conference room. I went to my office and prayed. "Now, Lord I need your help. Why did you give me this job and have the State come on my 5th day on the job. I just completed orientation. I need your help."

The State visit was superb. The organization passed with no recommendation. I understood that this was the first time this had happened. During the State review, one of the reviewers invited me to join their team as an Employee of the State. This I declined as this was not the will of the Lord for me.

I was beginning to learn to lean not to my own understanding. God spoke to my heart. He said, "I will never leave you or forsake you. I just want you to know who I am".

Let your conversation be without covetousness; and be content with such things as ye have: for he hath said, I will never leave thee, nor forsake thee. So that we may boldly say, The Lord is my helper, and I will not fear what man shall do unto me

(Hebrews 13:5-6)

I thought God you are all right. God simply wanted me to know that He could give me a job and a better one than the one I had. In spite of the many blessings I was receiving, a new job, God bringing me through a favorable inspection, I was still planning my retaliation on the institution and the doctor, but God reminded me to trust Him.

Humans are only the instruments, which God uses, such as the doctors and the hospital to move me forward to His will. Do not be mad at the Judases of this world. Only thing to do when the die is cast is to pray. Pray for wisdom, discernment and patience as you wait for God to reveal Himself in the total situation. Follow God's instructions.

After a year in the current management position, I was interviewed for and accepted a teaching position with the State of Florida. I was accepted for the position prior to completion of my application for the job. I know God was speaking to me loud and clear. I received a call and was told to go to the school board and fill out an application. I was technically hired before I even applied. That is how magnificent God is.

"I don't know why someone with a Doctorate of Philosophy degree would be accepting a high school teaching position. Why not teach at a college or the university, why a high school?" My family and friends inquired. All I could say was, "I am following His direction." I asked for His guidance, now I must trust Him.

It just didn't make sense. I was not only teaching at a high school with a doctorate degree but I was also offered less money. The more I prayed about this the stronger the affirmation from God.

Trust in the LORD with all thine heart; and lean not unto thine own understanding. (Proverbs 3:5.)

Little did I know what God had in store for me.

In the same the year I began teaching school, I was offered the position of supply pastor for a local church. God was taking me where He wanted me to go. He not only opened the door for great ministry as servant leader but He increased my salary. The pay cut that I took as a teacher was given back to me two-fold as a supply pastor. I was given flexibility in my teaching schedule that allowed me to meet the needs of the church without stress or duress. God blesses and adds no sorrow. I was able to retire with a Florida State pension with the number of years desired plus I was enrolled in a new pension plan with the church.

The blessing of the LORD, it makes rich,
and he adds no sorrow with it.

(Proverbs 10:22).

In God's way and God's time, according to His plan, what I prayed for I received. When the die is cast – go with God.

Yielding to God's will and way requires self-discipline, much faith and much prayer.

"Forgive us our d as we forgive our debtors"

(Matthew 9:12)

Chapter 7

My Pain

Forgive? How can I ever forgive? I may forgive but I will never forget. You cannot forgive without forgetting. As Jesus blots out our sins and casts them into the sea of forgetfulness so must we do to others who have trespassed against us.

My best friend, without my consent and knowledge, used my credit card to charge four sets of tires to my account. Quite naturally I was hurt, disappointed and wanted to retaliate. In fact, I extracted some money from her deceitfully. She used my credit card without permission. She charged four sets of car tires to my account and forged my name.

Upon receiving the bill, I called her up and demanded the $500 immediately. After receiving the cash I demanded she to go to the store and pay them or else I would call the police. She complied and paid the store as well. What an act of retaliation. I felt justified.

Did I forgive my friend? No, I did just the opposite. I fed her with a long handle spoon. But, it did not seem to deter her actions of deceit. At church she continued to do little underhanded things. In fact, at the time, my husband and I were having marital conflict, she called and asked me when was I going to give my husband a divorce so they could get married? I informed her she would be the first to know.

I tell you I had a very difficult time with this one. Forgiveness was not in my vocabulary. Yes, I was saved. Yes, I prayed the Lord's Prayer. Yes, I said, 'Forgive me my trespasses, as I forgive those who trespass against me.' I wanted forgiveness but was not willing to extend the same mercy to others.

A need for revenge was mounting. I was preoccupied with the thought of vengeance. I talked about nothing else in my conversation with others. I was seeking support in my evil thinking. There were many "good Christians" who supported my battle cry of "revenge", but thanks be to God for a praying mother in the church. She called me aside and spoke to me in love. She said, "You are the one to whom God is speaking; you need to show love and forgiveness."

Just as the prophet Nathan spoke to David she spoke to me. (Read 2 Samuel 12:1-7).

She helped me understand that un-forgiveness became my pain. There is a real burden that un-forgiveness places on the soul, mind, and body. Jesus taught the disciples "For if ye forgive men their trespasses, your heavenly Father will also forgive you: But if ye forgive not men their trespasses, neither will your Father forgive your trespasses." (Matthew. 6:14-15).

Jesus wants us to acknowledge that although we may not have trespassed against the one who trespassed against us, we all trespass on a daily basis. Like David, I had sinned against God. (2 Samuel 12:13). I had to pray and seek God for mercy to wash and cleanse me from my evil thoughts toward that person. (Psalm 51:1-9).

Believe me when I tell you that God's grace moved me to a new level. I was able to embrace my sister and to love her in spite of her deceit and the pain she inflicted. I pray for her daily asking God to draw her closer so that she too can learn to love unconditionally. For when we love, we do not hurt. Through this prayer I was set free. The act of forgiving cleanses and heals.

"Be you therefore merciful as your Father also is merciful!"

(Luke 6:36).

"…Let your supplication be made known unto God'

(Philippians 4:6)

Chapter 8

My Cry

"Are you sure doctor? Are the test result accurate or should we do them again?" He responded, "I am sorry. You will not be able to have children. All of the test we ran give the same results." Have you and your husband considered adoption?

There was no earthly reason for us to have had that discussion. All of my sisters were quite fertile. One had eight children and another five. Every one of my siblings had at least one child. Life is just not fair. I love children. I would keep all five of my oldest sister's children. Children were and still are the joy of my life. They are gifts from God.

I began to question God and plead my case. "Oh, God, why would you withhold this gift from me?" "What have I done wrong?" "I have tried to please you in every way I could, yet I am told I will never have children." I remembered how Hanna prayed so fervently in the temple that the priest thought she was drunk. Like Hannah I began to lay it before God.

After five years of marriage and no children, people were beginning to talk. They were like Peninnah (1 Samuel 1-40) taunting me in what they called a "Christian" way, questioning, "When are you all going to start a family?" "Don't you think it's time to start that family?" Then there were the statements, "Don't' wait too long now to get pregnant', and "You are not getting any younger". We would have loved to have had little juniors running around our church, but God had not gifted us yet. People can pierce the soul with well-meaning statements, however, if people only knew the agony of the unbridled tongue.

In the Bible days not having children was a sign of one that is cursed or not highly favored by God. Children were considered a blessing. I did not feel un-favored by God, but I wondered why His grace was not abundant enough to open my womb. "Father just one, just give me one fruit of the womb." I prayed earnestly and fasted frequently. During one of my visits home, I confided in my sister again. Together we sought the face of God. She took me to an elder's house. This elder was a prayer warrior and prophetess.

Upon leaving her house she said, "Your womb will be opened."

A few months later, I began to feel sick to my stomach. This was abnormal for me; rarely did I ever get sick. The morning sickness became unbearable. I went to see a doctor. By this time I had missed a menstrual period and was beginning to think I might be pregnant.

The doctor had heard all the community gossip about my home life. He told me the sickness and the menstrual absence was indeed signs of stress. He prescribed medications to help me deal with "my stress." Praise be to God I did not lean to my own understanding. I went before God acknowledging Him and His promised word that if we ask we will receive if we do not ask amiss. As I prayed I kept hearing the words, "Whose report will you believe?" I got off my knees and said, "Lord I believe your report. The devil is a "liar". In spite of the results I received from the tests and professional advice, I believe you Lord. I know you will answer my prayers.

I went to the drug store after talking with my friend and bought a pregnancy kit. The results showed positive for pregnancy. I made an appointment with another gynecologist. Test results at his office were positive for pregnancy. Be fervent and persistent in prayers. God may not answer when or how you want, but He will answer according to His will. Seven months later I gave birth to my first born son. Five years later I gave birth to my second son. God is able to do above all that we ask or think.

> *"Now unto him that is able to do exceeding abundantly above all that we ask or think, according to the power that works in us..."*
>
> *(Ephesians: 3:20)*

"Set your affection on things above,
not on things on the earth."

(Colossians 3:2)

Chapter 9

My Desperation

My situation at home had become so bleak, I was afraid to answer the doorbell. I never knew if it was the re-possessors for the furniture or someone coming in person to collect their money." Bill collectors were constantly calling the house about financial obligations I was unaware of and for which I was unable to provide answers.

One morning there was a loud boisterous knocking at the door. I opened the door to find a man who said, "Your husband said you have the $3,000 for me." "Sir, I have no idea what you are talking about. I do not have $3,000 dollars." In fact I had no money at that time. God was truly on my side. This tough looking, gentleman was very angry because obviously he had been given the run around and was sent to me to collect his money. This was a tactic for delaying payment to individuals owed. Talk about being frightened! It was a very terrifying experience. The gentleman, in spite of his demeanor, was very kind to me and accepted my word.

You want to know about financial planning, bill collectors, and the laws that govern them? Ask me about dodging phone calls and not answering the door. Our bills were insurmountable. I believe in honesty. To me not paying a bill is stealing, getting something for nothing. It is lying when we fail to keep our part of the covenant or agreement.

We had three incomes in our household. I was working two jobs and he had one. However, only two came home. I was struggling and could see no way out. The two paychecks I brought home were not sufficient to cover all the bills. I paid the essentials, but was bound by marriage to bills that were not mine. God knows I needed help. I kept asking God what to do. I sought the financial planners, the money managers, but the burden of increased financial obligations continued. I could stand it no longer. I was about to lose my mind.

I prayed the prayer of desperation. 'Help me Jesus. I need you Lord. Help me. I do not know what to do.

Come Jesus. Come quickly.' Seems the more I prayed the worse things got. I found out about more bills. My personal credit card, which I never used, had over $7,000 worth of charges. The company was calling me regarding payment. My checking account was over drawn by $700 for checks, I never wrote. It was just too much. I needed direction.

God always comes through for His children. The favor of God had the bank replace my money due to erroneous signature. The credit card company was able to trace the charges and remove them from my account. I was released from the obligation of paying for debt I had not accumulated. And, I left court from my divorce proceeding debt-free. God in His own time and in His own way will give you direction. He will bring relief. He will give courage to face the unknown.

My outer nature was wasting away but my inner nature was being renewed every day. God was strengthening me in the midst of this financial crisis. He moved me to a debt-free life. I praise God I do not have to beg, borrow, or steal. I know how to wait on God for anything my heart desires. He strengthened me and empowered me in self-discipline and patience. I am a living witness He will set you free and break any chains that bind you.

I don't know what struggles you might be having right now, but do what God has asked you to do. He asks that in all things we seek Him. He will direct our paths. God will break bad habits. He will remove you from bad situations. He will change situations. He is able to do above and beyond anything we can ask. Prayer moves His hands in further work for His children.

Now unto him that is able to do exceeding abundantly above all that we ask or think, according to the power that worketh in us,

(Ephesians 3:20)

Chapter 10

Position Yourself.

In every situation God has worked for me. When I called out to Him He has answered. I wouldn't know what to do if it was not for the Lord God almighty. I have listed a few of the things that brought me to my knees, but time and space would not allow me to tell you about my cancer diagnosis, the challenges of ministry, the many dark nights of the soul, nor dark days of despair. But in my darkest hours, I cried unto the Lord and He heard my cry. He came and saw about me.

Perhaps you were one of the persons God sent. Perhaps you knew my situation and were one of the persons who simply prayed for me; or maybe you were just an encouraging angel along the way. To you

I say, "Thank you." I found out that when I called on God He answered by dispatching angels to defend and to take care of me. I praise God for the angels in my life. I have never called Him and He did not answer. Sometimes He came right away, sometimes He seemed to delay answering, but one thing I can say with certainty – He always came right on time. He still comes on time.

There were times I couldn't get to my knees. It was a crisis situation so I would call Him standing, sitting, riding, bent over or lying down. When a crisis hits we forget about appearances, we forget about protocol and we institute emergency measures. God answers those prayers as well. God hears the hearts of his children. Our hearts will direct our posture. Do not get hung up on the physical position. If you are in the wrong position He will let you know. God simply wants you to call Him. Talk to Him for when we talk to God, He will direct our steps. He will give us peace and comfort. He will reassure us that He is still on the throne, in charge, and has not forgotten us.

At times I have found myself almost leveled to the ground. But when I went into prayer, God lifted me up and I couldn't do anything else but praise him! He is a Lifter! Destructive weapons may be hurled at you, but they will not succeed. They just won't work against the power of God.

My prayer of praise to God destroyed the enemy's weapons of mass destruction. Praise will open the heavens and cause God's blessings to flow down. Just remember we are in spiritual warfare and we need to attack from whatever position would best destroy the enemy.

Sometimes the enemy is better attacked
from a lay low position.

."...whatever things you ask in prayer,
believing, you will receive."

(Matthew 21:22).

*"…Whatever things you ask in prayer,
believing, you will receive."*

(Matthew 21:22)

Chapter 11

A Weapon of Mass Destruction

Prayer is a weapon of great power. Prayer is so powerful that the powerful hates it. They try to remove it and many abandon it. If people weren't afraid of prayer they would leave it alone. It poses a major problem for many.

When faced with potential life-threatening situations we must ask the question, "Whose report are you going to believe?" God can overrule a doctor's diagnosis of cancer and the prognosis of short or poor life expectancy. I can list a number of persons who have been given a terminal diagnosis with a projected life span. But when they turned their face to the wall and cried out to God in prayer like Hezekiah, God healed them. " I have heard thy prayer, I have seen thy tears: behold, I will heal thee . . . And I will add unto thy days fifteen years . . ." (2 King 20:5-6). Prayer is a mighty weapon. "Trust in the Lord with all your heart, and lean not on your own understanding; in all your ways acknowledge Him, and He shall direct your paths." (Proverbs 3:5-6).

We predict no rain, but yet rain comes after a statewide call to prayers. I do not know how prayer works, but I can tell you it does indeed. I have prayed for my children, I have prayed for my healing, yes God healed and delivered me.

When we pray:

- **Power and Authority are released.** Prayer is so powerful it does what surgeons cannot do. Surgeons can perform heart transplants that repair the physical need. But prayer changes the total person. David asked for a new heart and he received it. "Create in me a clean heart Oh God; and renew a right spirit within me." (Psalms 51: 10).
  - **Removes barriers**. It will remove the bars of hatred and pride. Peter said, "Not so, Lord; for I have never eaten anything that is common or unclean." (Acts 10:14).
  - **Gives wisdom**. King Solomon prayed for

wisdom and was able to solve social and human dilemmas. (1 Kings 3: 16-28).

- **Transforms society.** When the hearts of people change, society change. Laws, even though they are needed to keep us from being the Wild West, do not and cannot solve our social dilemmas. They simply suppress some people's behavior for a time. Notice there are more laws, but also more jails today than ever before. Change comes when the heart is transformed through the sanctifying blood of Jesus. This occurs when we pray. (2 Chronicles 7:14)

- **Brings healing.** Blind Bartimeaus cried out to Jesus asking to receive his sight. Jesus healed him. (Mark 10: 46-52). The Word tells us, "When you are sick send for the elders of the church..." (James 5:14)

- **Provides strength –** Keeps us in the midst of struggles. Gives divine comfort and rest as we meditate on the promises of God.

- **Moves the hands of God.** Peter was supernaturally released from jail. The people at the prayer meeting were astounded that their prayers had been answered. The young lady answered Peter's knock and told the prayer band that Peter was at the door they did not believe her. "So Peter was kept in prison, but the church was earnestly praying to God for him." (Read Acts 12:1-16). It baffles our intellect and confounds modern science. Prayers do what nothing else and no one else can do. It moves the hands of God.

Prayer is available to all that believe. We can call on anytime and anywhere. Paul encourages us to pray without ceasing. It is our greatest weapon to defeat the enemy. Christians, we are called to destroy the enemy, to shoot him down with cries to heaven. The power of prayer is like an underground current or an electric current of lightening that reveals the power of God. No official power can stop or hamper its' effect. It is a mystery, a phenomenon. Therefore, pray without ceasing.

"Men ought always to pray, and not to faint."

(Luke 18:1).

The prayer of a righteous man availeth much.

(James 5:16)

More things are wrought by prayers
than this world ever dreams off

(a quote from -Alfred, Lord Tennyson)

Chapter 12

Pray Always

The Conclusion of the whole matter: Humans are to pray without ceasing. It is the Christians' weapon to fight the forces of evil and to overcome through Jesus Christ. My prayer is that your life would become a life of prayer. Pray until something happens. Pray until Christ returns. Until His kingdom come on earth as it is in heaven.

As you live a life of prayer you will find that prayers not only changes things but prayer empowers us to fight the good fight and to be victorious. Therefore as you keep your priorities right; your hearts will be open to our unlimited resources in Christ. I pray that as you talk with God He will overshadow you with wisdom and discernment.

I exhort you therefore to make supplications for all people, especially those of the household of faith, that we might be strengthened in the power and might of God. I exhort you to wage war with the tools of the Christian trade – Prayer. It is our most powerful weapon for warfare.

Praying always with all prayer and supplication in the Spirit, being watchful to this end with all perseverance and supplication for all the saints. (Ephesians 6:18).

Therefore I exhort first of all that supplications, prayers, intercessions, and giving of thanks be made for all men, for kings and all who are in authority, that we may lead a quiet and peaceable life in all godliness and reverence. (1st Timothy 2:1-2).

"For by one Spirit are we all baptized into one body, whether we be Jews or Gentiles, whether we be bond or free; and have been all made to drink into one Spirit."
(1 Corinthians 12:13.)

I exhort you to wage war with the tools of the Christian trade – Prayer. It is our most powerful weapon for warfare.

"Let us therefore come boldly to the throne of grace, that we may obtain mercy and find grace to help in time of need."

(Hebrews 4:16).

A Prayer

Oh loving God, let your people know the value and power of prayer. Give us grace to use this weapon that you have so graciously given to us. Grant us love to share with others the blessedness of your love and care.

Teach us to keep you as the source of our strength, so we may rise above the challenges of this life. Grant us wisdom to rely on your word and let prayer become the foremost and most important part of our daily lives.

Keep us faithful to your word, relying on the truth of it and help us to make it a lamp unto our feet and the light of our path. Whatever may befall us may we continue looking to the hills from whence comes our help.

May we never cease to use the gift of prayer and even

when all seem lost or impossible help us to know that this mighty weapon is effective and that you always hear and answer prayer.

This I ask in the name of Jesus Christ, our Lord and Savior.
Amen

"And the very God of peace sanctify you wholly;
and I pray God your whole spirit and soul
and body be preserved blameless unto the
coming of our Lord Jesus Christ."

(1 Thessalonians 5:23)

Practical Application

Here are five practical steps on how to get started
using the tool to create your Prayer Life:

STEP 1: **Devote** a few minutes of each day for
prayer.

STEP 2: **Develop A Discipline of Prayer.** Pray for
two minutes a day, increase gradually to
five and continue to increase the time you
set aside. Soon, you will be praying for
long periods without it becoming a strain.

The more you become disciplined in your prayer life you will find it not just a habit but a joy.

STEP 3:   **Give Praise and Thanks.** Pray the Word. Praise God for who He is and for what He has done.

The Book of Psalms is a good place to start. There are great prayers of praise and thanksgiving in the Psalms.

- I will bless the Lord at all times (Psalms 34:1)
- O, give thanks unto the Lord for He is good (Psalms 118:1).
- Give thanks to the Lord, call on His Name; make known among the nations what He has done. Sing to Him, sing praise to Him; tell of all His wonderful acts. Glory in His holy Name; let the hearts of those who seek the Lord rejoice. Look to the Lord and His strength; seek His Face always. (Psalm 105:1–4).
- "How great is your goodness, which you have stored up for those who fear you, which you bestow in the sight of men on those who take refuge in you." (Psalm 31:19).

- Give thanks unto the LORD; for he is good: for his mercy endureth forever. (Psalms 136:1)

Prayers of praise and thanksgiving draw us closer into God's presence. They remind us of and give us insight into who God is. Prayers of thanksgivings initiate an attitude of gratitude and give us a humble spirit.

STEP 4: **Ask** --Petition God for your hearts desire. Be specific about what you want. Pray for transformation. ". . . present your bodies a living sacrifice. . . be ye transformed by the renewing of your mind. . ." (Romans 12:1).

- My heart's desire is to have the mind of Christ. Let this mind be in you, which was also in Christ Jesus. (Philippians 2:5). Tell God about your heart's desire tell Him what you want.
- Pray that this day you will be strengthened to avoid the company of those who will cause you to walk in the flesh. Pray to have fellowship with those who can help you make the right decision. Pray not to listen to bad advice or counsel and to be governed by the word of God. (Psalms 1).

- Paul prayed "...that I might know Him and the power of his resurrection." (Philippians 3:10) and you can ask this also.
- The apostles asked, "And the apostles said unto the Lord, Increase our faith." (Luke 17:5). If you need an increase of faith ask.
- The blind man asked for sight he began to cry out, and say, "Jesus, you son of David, have mercy on me!" ... "Rhabboni, **that I may see again**." (Read Mark 10:46-52).

Prayers of petition recognizes the almighty power of God; shows our dependency on Him and brings a realization that whatever we ask in His name will be granted according to His will.

STEP 5: Intercede for Others.

- Jesus prayed for His disciples. (John 17) *"I am not praying for the world, but for those you have given me, for they are yours."*
- Paul prayed for the Ephesians. (Ephesians 1:16–19) *"Cease not to give thanks for you, making mention of you in my prayers . . ."*
- Paul prayed for Philemon. (Philemon 1: 25) *"The grace of our Lord Jesus Christ be with your spirit. Amen."*
- Timothy urges intercession. (1 Timothy 2:1-2) *"I urge, then, first of all, that requests,*

*prayers, intercession and thanksgiving be made
for everyone . . . "*

Prayers of petition remind us of the many
people who are praying for the household
of faith and that we are not alone in our
struggles. There are angels all around
praying for us as we pray for others.

As you pray the Word your prayers will became more
and more spiritual and less temporal. Pray for the
mind of Christ Jesus to be the mind that is in you and
soon *your life will become a life of prayer*

Pray the Word

Lest We Forget

Keep a prayer Journal. A prayer journal helps us to record God's responses to our prayers in the past, acknowledge what He is doing in the present, and gives us assurance for the future.

A Prayer Journal:
- Keeps us focus on what we want God to do for us and in us.
- Helps us to enumerate and count our blessings
- Gives insight into the quality and quantity of our prayer requests
- Lets us know whether our praise out number our requests

- Gives us hope and assurance
- Affirm that God answers prayers
- In the midst of struggles we can look back at the past and see what God has done and we can hold to our faith that God will answer.

When we use a prayer journal we will find that our blessings far outweigh our struggles and we will praise and give thanks. When we count our blessings we will truly be surprised at what God has already done.

God is able to do more than we can ever think to ask of Him. He saw my struggle, heard my cry, felt my pain and gave me deliverance. Prayer has been the tool that has worked for me. Try it. It has been my most powerful weapon. It destroyed my fears, built my faith, and has kept me in constant contact with my Father. Don't stop praying. Pray until something happens *(PUSH)*. Storm the gates with prayers.

"And pray in the Spirit on all occasions with all kinds of prayers and requests. With this in mind, be alert and always keep on praying for all the saints."

(Ephesians 6:18).

References:

Boston Globe: www.mindpowernews.com/**Prayer** *For Healing.htm*

www.npr.org/templates/story/story. php?storyId=16281915 In Drought-Stricken Georgia, a Prayer for Rain by Kathy Lohr NPR Morning edition.

Douglas, J.D., Ed., "New Commentary on the Whole Bible: New Testament Volume," Tyndale House Pub., (1990)

Howell, F., Ph.D. " Dear God I Want To Be Rich"

I. Asimov, "Asimov's Guide to the Bible", Wings Books, New York NY, (1981)

Kenneth Stevenson, "Abba Father: Understanding and Using the Lord's Prayer," Canterbury Press, (2000), Page 27. <u>Read reviews or order this book safely from Amazon.com online book store</u>

Laymon, C.M., Ed., "Interpreter's One Volume Commentary on the Bible", Abingdon Press, Nashville TN (1971).

"PC Study Bible: Matthew Henry's Commentary", Biblesoft, Seattle WA (1994)

Scripture taken from the HOLY BIBLE, NEW INTERNATIONAL VERSION®. Copyright © 1973, 1978, 1984 Biblica. Used by permission of Zondervan. All rights reserved.

"Scripture taken from the New King James Version. Copyright © 1982 by Thomas Nelson, Inc. Used by permission. All rights reserved."

The United Methodist Hymnal, Copyright ©1989 (Third printing) The United Methodist Publishing house (Page 130).

Wesley, J.: The Great Methodist © 1997 by Sam Wellman Published by Barbour Publishing, Inc., Urichsville, Ohio.